Five Dreams

All rights reserved. No part of this publication may be reproduced, distributed, or transmitted in any form by any means, including photocopying, recording, or other electronic methods without the prior written permission of the author, except in the case of brief quotations embodied in reviews and certain other noncommercial uses permitted by copyright law. For permission requests, write to the author at the email address below.

Copyright © 2023 Elizabeth Michaud

emichpoet@gmail.com

979-8-9887275-0-7

Cover Art & Design by Tell Tell Poetry
Edited by Tell Tell Poetry

Printed in the United States of America

First Printing, 2023

For my three great loves, my children:
Sara, Stella, and Ben.

CONTENTS

I DREAM OF YOU

For Him	5
Infatuation	6
Summoner's Dance	7
Stop Toying with Me	8
As Sting Is My Witness	10
Have No Doubt	11
The Proposal	12
Of Love & Woe	13
Torn	14
Lovers as the Gods Intended	17
An (Alliterative) Affair	19
Of Bitter Dreams & Slumber	21
This Breach Is Only Temporary	22
Come Back	24

I DREAM OF TWINS

Old Tree	29
Old Tree Begs Forgiveness	31
My Statue of Liberty, Part I	33
My Statue of Liberty, Part II	35
A Book, a Tome, and an Escapade	37
A Train, a Circus, and a Flight of Fancy	38
Quest	40

Quest Aborted	41
love travels on, part one: her	43
love travels on, part two: him	44
White Walls, Part I	45
White Walls, Part II	47
Wife	49
Spring Cleaning	50

I DREAM OF SORROW

For Tante Cecelle	55
Requiem for a Wake	57
Put Flowers on My Grave	59
The Meaningless Process of Goodbye	61
Too Little, Too Late	62
The Wish of a Battered Soul	63
Once in Faith	64
Grief Unrelenting	66
Grief of Ghosts	67

I HAVE STRANGE DREAMS

In the Eye of the Heavenly Storm	73
To the Wind with Gratitude	74
Grave Digger	75
Faculty Meeting	77
Accident	79

She Walks the Gravel Road	80
Sightless	81
There's Poetry Everywhere	82
You Talk of Freedom	84
Tragic Lies	86
A Summer Gathering	88

NIGHTMARES

Ghost	93
The Wind Is His Messenger	95
Let the Sounds be a Warning	97
The Naming of Her	99
The Devil's Harlot	101
Black Widow	102
Rat	104
Intruder	106
And an Angel Will Lead Him Home	109
Last Words	110

FIVE DREAMS

I DREAM OF YOU

ELIZABETH MICHAUD

FOR HIM

There is an art to waiting patiently.
It is grace in restraint and calm in expectation,
and there is a virtuosity in wanting without receiving,
strength in denial, fortitude in disappointment.
And so it is with longing,
that curious emotion between patience and desire,
that resides in the most tender part of the soul,
unresolved, unsettled,
but achingly beautiful, nonetheless.

INFATUATION

take these reckless sighs I breathe
and this weakness in my knees
take this lurid sideways glance
these giddy words of happenstance
take this wetness between my thighs
take these shudders from my spine
take these tingles in my limbs
and passion's promise from within
take my heart and its rapid beat
take this warm blush from my cheeks
take this quiver from my lips
and these secrets from my hips
take all these bits and parts of me
take them all and love me
love me

ELIZABETH MICHAUD

SUMMONER'S DANCE

When once my love I wished to see,
but longest night kept him from me.
I took a chance to dance about,
with spin and twirl I cast night out.
The light of moon I drained away,
rid sky of stars without delay.
I dismissed dark with wave of hand,
dispelled night's mist away from land.
Like this I turned the night to day;
like this I saw time melt away.
The sun in sky did beckon rise,
and mortal men did so oblige.
And once again I found him here,
next to my heart, so near and dear.

FIVE DREAMS

STOP TOYING WITH ME

Hey, Clock,
I see the games you play,
taking your sweet time while you
make me wait
for him.
Oh yeah, Clock, I'm talking to you,
you and your boys....
I saw what Minutehand did:
strolled between four and five,
stopped to chat
(plotted against six, seven, and eight, I'm sure),
the nerve....
And Secondhand is no better—
decided he'd play *Minutehand*
by making seconds to minutes—
even as I watched.
It's a treachery, a total betrayal—
And Hourhand? He's the worst.
Chimed the hour delayed on purpose,
but when I'm late for work,
he can't move fast enough,
and when I need a little extra sleep,
he's right there—early even.

Yeah, Clock, I'm mad at
you and your cohorts 'cause you know me,
and you know I'm
missing him,
        needing him,
                wanting him,
but you play your games with me
and make me wait
for him.

AS STING IS MY WITNESS

I'm an Englishman in New York
searching for signs of the apocalypse
(or maybe just hints of a small upcoming disaster),
but there are no signs,
and the evidence is clear:
history will teach us nothing.
Maybe losing you is inevitable,
because I know
how fragile this love is,
but seven days without you
is like a dagger straight to my heart.
I want to forget about the future
and live in this here and in this now
with you, my desert rose
on a brand-new day,
a lithium sunset as our background
because I'm mad about you.

HAVE NO DOUBT

and when it's all been exhausted
the endlessness of infinity
the perpetuity of forever
the boundlessness of eternity
and *still* a second should remain
for you I'll steal the glow of moon from the bleakest night
I'll kidnap the shade of trees on the hottest day
and I'll plunder the crash of waves from the stormiest of seas
lest you should ever wonder
if I loved you

FIVE DREAMS

THE PROPOSAL

It is a slow work, making the right hand
and the left hand come together. Tedious, but
patience is a virtue, and so is passion.
The metronome is a relentless teacher, persistent, and
demands obedience. It will *tick tick tick*
its instruction, and fingers will slide
over yellowed ivory keys once, twice, a dozen times,
a hundred times.
By the glow of an antique gaslight,
a melody will take shape.
It will slip out the crack of the open window
and float on fog and mist.
Cleverly, spontaneously, he'll use it
to set the mood, and on a night
where stars like pearls from a broken necklace are
scattered in the sky,
he'll profess his love for her.

ELIZABETH MICHAUD

OF LOVE & WOE

When oft I wished for word of kind,
his words to me were oft unkind.
When with fervor I sought caress,
his touch to me brought grief and stress.
When I desired charity,
an open hand—humanity!
He turned from me, hand closed in fist, with no regard—malevolence!
And when I longed for happiness, for ecstasy, for sweet, sweet bliss—
      Oh, my love, my king, my prince—
to me, he brought unhappiness.

FIVE DREAMS

TORN

I think of him
but I dream of you
I hold his hand
but your touch is true
his lips touch mine
but you kiss me sweet—
        my knees do tremble
        I'm unsteady on my feet

I am his equal
but for you I'm a slave
he'd die for me
but I'll dig your grave
he is my knowledge
but you are my truth—
        constant, definite
        you're absolute

He sees my love
but you know my passion
he wants me to focus
but you're my distraction
he brings me chocolate
but you're my dessert—
        sweet and delicious
        I'll taste of you first

ELIZABETH MICHAUD

To him I'm a saint
but you know I'm your angel
to him I'm just naughty
you know I'm a devil
I make him mad
but you drive me insane—
        oh yes my love
          it's you who's to blame

He bathes in my love
but with you I'm immersed
I whet his palate
but you quench my thirst
he fights the good fight
but you've battled for me—
        waged war with men
        sent ships out to sea

He whispers his words
you romance me with verse
I scold him gently
but you and I curse
I ask him nicely
but with you I plead—
        I beg I beseech
        it's you that I need

FIVE DREAMS

I shield him from darkness
but you light my night
I'm the heat of his sun
you're a warm ray of light
he gives me shelter
but you are my home—
    with you in this sanctum
    I'm never alone

He misses me fondly
when I am gone
but my heart aches for you
I'm lost and withdrawn
I lay with him
but for you I lust—
    your hot tight embrace
    each powerful thrust

He walks on firm ground
but you rise above
he is my lover
but you are my love
he is my lifeline
but you're my salvation—
    my deliverance my rescue
    my sweet liberation

My man he is
but your woman I'd be—
take witness, oh love
of this cruel travesty

ELIZABETH MICHAUD

LOVERS AS THE GODS INTENDED

I'll seduce you if you let me
and you'll be made to see
the love you seek so pure and true
in me rests softly deep
And even when my heart moves on
to another man
I'll bide my time until you call
extend to you my hand

And when her love turns bitter
and she remembers not
how you once proclaimed your love for her
it twisted you in knots
For you I'll bring salvation
how wondrous is my love
I'll whisper softly sweet to you
and we shall rise above

The loves we've known will disappear
and fade from this existence
We'll find each other once again
and melt away the distance
        There will be no more resistance
The hands of time will rotate back
our lives will start anew
lovers as the gods intended
and bliss shall we pursue

The passion that my heart has known
has yet to pass or die
of you I think when sorrow calls
the loss does not subside
      My desire still resides
and I'll gladly leave the one I'm with
to have you by my side

AN (ALLITERATIVE) AFFAIR

I'm his forbidden fantasy
his Friday night fancy
his release from reality
his filthy flirtation
his unfulfilled frustration
And he's my secret sensation
my salacious stimulation
my escape to elation
my mantra my meditation
He's my world my country
my naughty nation

And when we cast the world aside
we come together
insatiable in our infatuation
impervious to the implications
oblivious to our obligations
We're going to the next elevation
it's a luscious levitation (but God knows I
yield to him in supplication)

And on this platform of pleasure
it's tranquil it's treasure
without any pressure
this love without measure
It's passion prohibited
but we're uninhibited
by desire unlimited and
romance revisited

FIVE DREAMS

It's excitement and ecstasy
Oh relentless chemistry
I'm his siren his seductress
he's my idol my Adonis

And in quiet places
with secluded spaces
we keep our union undercover
(we keep our union under covers)
as discreetly we discover
this wondrous world of
secret lovers

OF BITTER DREAMS & SLUMBER

Leave me for a fortnight,
invade my dreams no more;
let me slumber with a stillness
disturbed by you no more.
Double now your absence,
increase the fortnight still by two,
your presence in my sleeping state
will simply never do.
I cannot stand for this grim action,
this betrayal of mind and heart,
for daylight will remind me
we'll forever be apart;
you belong now to another,
on her hand, she wears your ring,
so spare me this injustice
for you no longer are my king—
so I'll beg of you again:
wander not into my sleep!
If you'll not be mine in day,
then love at night we shall not keep—
because this dream of love
upon the morn is oft untrue;
'tis but a trick you would employ
that my passion would stay true.
So on my knees, I will beseech you,
and dreams of you I will "Be gone!"
I'll embrace my sleep, seek some peace
and wish my heart to carry on.

THIS BREACH IS ONLY TEMPORARY

You're on my mind
like you sometimes are,
kidnapping my thoughts.
You sneak in,
as if I've left a back door open,
left it slightly ajar.
I don't hear it creak.
No, just a gentle push on the knob
and you slip right in.
You don't knock, you enter,
unannounced and uninvited,
unwanted.

You're on my mind
like you sometimes are,
stealing my attention.
You creep in,
as if I've left a window open,
high in its frame
for the breeze to blow through,
and you in the wind.
You tousle my thoughts
and stir up my memories,
unbidden and unasked,
unwelcome.

You're on my mind
like you sometimes are,
capturing my hopes.

ELIZABETH MICHAUD

You slink in,
as if I've left the basement open,
the foundation of my soul
laid bare to your torment.
You seek to undo me,
but I'll be victorious over you yet.
The doors will shut,
the window will close,
and I'll be free again.

COME BACK

In this lifetime
and into the next
I'll write a thousand words of sadness
scribble a hundred verses of regret
sing a million songs of anguish
and spill countless tears of remorse
I'll imagine infinite dreams of sorrow
breathe endless sighs of discontent
ponder a billon thoughts of woe
in this lifetime
and into the next
and in all these things I'll wish
I never let you go

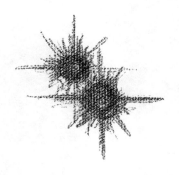

I DREAM OF TWINS

ELIZABETH MICHAUD

OLD TREE

Old tree
dark tree sinister tree
I know 'bout you
and them secrets you like to keep
behind leaves so green
and flowers so fresh
but that ain't nothing but lies and falsehoods
'cause when the spring goes by
and that winter come
I see you for what you are
for what you done

That's right, Ol' Tree
with your branches bare
with your trunk scarred
you can't hide behind yo' leaves
you can't hide behind no *spring renewal*
'cause I know about you, Ol' Tree
what you done
what you hung
from branches so strong
they held the weight of a man
an innocent man
a black man

Oh yea I remember,
Ol' Tree
how you used to give us shade
used to keep us from the sun

FIVE DREAMS

when we made love
and you pretended you was our friend
our tree
but you was *his* tree
that white man's tree
and when that white man come
with that rope so thick
that rope so strong
you gave him a branch
you gave him an arm
and you let that white man steal a life,
Ol' Tree
you let him take my love

ELIZABETH MICHAUD

OLD TREE BEGS FORGIVENESS

Girl, I beg you, listen.
Autumn strips me of my leaves
so that winter can bare me naked to the world:
my scars exposed, my boughs twisted and gnarled,
my trunk haggard and wretched and ugly.
My sin is brought to witness.
I carried the weight of a man,
an innocent man—
a black man.

Girl, hear me, please!
This cold, harsh season reveals my guilt and shame:
the memory of his weight makes my branches sag,
my skeleton weak,
and I tremble when the wind blows.
I don't want to stand tall!
I wish for time to abuse me and
for nature to waste me
by flood or fire or both,
but God won't appease me
so here I am.

Girl, I beseech you, *please*!
Hear me while I make amends!
That springtime sun will
chase the ice away.
Don't be fooled by new leaves—
they won't hide no secrets!
For this dead man's grave,

FIVE DREAMS

my leaves will green and my flowers bloom
so we can remember
a black soul
that died in my unbidden arms
by a white man with a rope so thick,
a rope so strong,
who stole a life,
sweet girl,
and took your love.

ELIZABETH MICHAUD

MY STATUE OF LIBERTY, PART I

My Statue of Liberty
ain't no lady in green
sitting in a harbor
offerin' false promise
Not when *I'm* here
chained and shackled
and an old man's whip
is slashing my back

My Statue of Liberty
don't make false requests
like calling for "wretched souls
yearnin' to breathe free"
Not when *I'm* here
in the old man's field
choking on air
that stinks of bondage

My Statue of Liberty
wouldn't hold
no light of freedom
that I *can't* see
that don't lead me
Not when *I'm* here
runnin' in the dark
for my life
and that old man's dog
is hunting me

FIVE DREAMS

No sir
That ain't *my* statue
and her words ain't for me
Not when I'm here
swingin' from that old man's tree

ELIZABETH MICHAUD

MY STATUE OF LIBERTY, PART II

They be talkin' about a lady,
she got her hair done up in rows
but she hold her head up high
'cause there's somethin' that she knows.

They be talkin' about a lady,
she stand up tall and straight.
The masters, they don't like her none,
'cause she don't know "her place."

They be talkin' about a lady,
she got a light up in her hand.
Black folks say it's like a star
to lead 'em up out of this land.

They be talkin' about a lady,
she a friend to all us slaves:
she gonna get us out this misery,
we gonna see these end of days.

They be talkin' about a lady,
she standing for us all:
for them who fight for freedom,
for those who gonna fall.

They be talkin' about a lady,
she broke them shackles at her feet!
She hold 'em high up in the air,
it be a sign of victory.

FIVE DREAMS

They be talkin' about a lady,
made of stone up on the slope.
They say her name be Liberty
and she here to give us hope.

ELIZABETH MICHAUD

A BOOK, A TOME, AND AN ESCAPADE

When once I sought to travel far
and chance upon a foreign star,
or hear a tale of angst and woe,
or ladies quarrel o'er handsome beau—
I found a book of verse and rhyme,
a favorite tome to pass the time.
Off I went to Storyland,
where love was sweet, adventure grand,
and I was free to gallivant
among the tales that did enchant—
forever lost, forever free!
My soul filled with such harmony.
Until, alas! There came the end,
and there I was, at home again.

FIVE DREAMS

A TRAIN, A CIRCUS, AND A FLIGHT OF FANCY

From deepest slumber once I woke
upon a train of ancient oak;
'twas strange to find myself on board,
this odd event struck awkward chord.
With location unascertained,
with strange voyage unexplained,
I did remark with my own eyes
cargo of grand scope and size!
A king who sat upon a throne,
who wished that I might try a scone;
a maiden who contorted self;
an impish boy who seemed an elf.
Upon a wire, a man did walk,
and still another who seemed a hawk
(with pointed nose and beady eyes
no other words his look describes!).
A gypsy peered a crystal ball,
foretold the future of one and all;
a strongman raised a heavyweight;
plates of sweets a fat man ate.
And still my senses took in more:
the scent of popcorn and chocolate smores;
the roar of lions and greater beasts;
elephants that cried and screeched.
A barker pitched delights of tent,
with coins and bills, crowds gave consent,
and here I stood amongst it all,
upon this train, so much enthralled—

ELIZABETH MICHAUD

From deepest slumber, again I woke
upon a train of ancient oak.
My love was seated by my side
and with a twinkle in his eye,
he murmured his soft words to me:
"'Twas just a dream, go back to sleep."

QUEST

Seven poems in seven days—
I'll pursue this task without delay!
A lofty challenge for the mind,
but worry not! The words I'll find!
A verse of love will be the first
(that treach'rous emotion,
blessing and curse!).
A second day will bring remorse,
words of regret, wretched discourse.
Day three will find a dark, bleak rhyme—
a hint of terror would be sublime.
Next in queue: of nature's wrath,
of life beyond the aftermath.
On day five, words fall to chance;
I'll pen an ode of happenstance.
A lullaby awaits soon after,
to bring sweet sound of child's laughter.
(A whimsical tale with form and meter,
shall delight the youngest reader!)
The final day of this scribe's exertion,
brings somber notes of disconcertion:
of loss, of love, of blood, or death,
an opus to expel one's breath.
And with my quest for verse complete,
both thought and pen will find retreat.

ELIZABETH MICHAUD

QUEST ABORTED

They gave me seven days
to write my next great verse,
to put my pen to paper,
in words become immersed.
A week to write my tale,
to forge great lines with words and tone,
undisturbed by life's distractions
here in the quiet of my home.
Oh, seven days! Yes, seven days!
How I'm apt to fill the time,
with ode or prose or tale to spin,
this work should be sublime.
The clock will tick its passage
as I scribble, pen, and write
my greatest manifesto,
meant only to delight.
But as I sip a glass of wine
and the music softly plays,
the words are slipping from me
and the hours turn to days.
The quiet is a solace
and the peace brings comfort too;
the will to bring a tale to life
no longer does ring true.
My mind is wont to rest
and my spirit wander free.
Words and verse and prose and tale
will steal serenity.

FIVE DREAMS

So for seven days—oh seven days!
I'll take my leave of this scribe's chore
and grant interlude to find me,
that my spirit be restored.

ELIZABETH MICHAUD

LOVE TRAVELS ON, PART ONE: HER

the loneliest sound I've ever heard
is a train whistle blowing by
miserable and melancholy
floating on the cool crisp air
when morning is still night
and it's only me in this bed
'cause you're long gone
like that train racing by

LOVE TRAVELS ON, PART TWO: HIM

the sweetest sound I've ever heard
is a train whistle blowing by
like a promise of new fortune and liberation
it's providence
and on a cool crisp morning
pretending to be night
it lures me out
from between these sheets
and quick like that train passing by
I'm gone

ELIZABETH MICHAUD

WHITE WALLS, PART I

I hear the clock—it's ticking
it's counting down the time
The whispers that I hear
are converging in my mind
Their voices growing louder
and I miss the bright blue sky
The promise of tomorrow
shattered by a lullaby—
By the sweetest song of madness
and my mind will soon descend
from the light into the darkness
I wish to comprehend—
But the fields where I roamed free
and the ocean where I stepped
are soon to be no more to me
as I make this new descent—
The clock is ticking louder
and in my head the voices rise
They sing a song of chaos
and it's coming from all sides
And as I step out from the sunshine
into the dark of night
into a bleak despair
which is soon to be my right—
My time in light is ending
and my life of old is gone
where flowers flourished in my hands
and my will was done—

FIVE DREAMS

And the clock has run its course
The time has now run out
They've come to take me from my home
For them there is no doubt
    The voices carry all the clout—
White walls now surround me
I'm trapped and I'm encaged
They tell me that my mind is gone
And all that's left is fear and rage

ELIZABETH MICHAUD

WHITE WALLS, PART II

The whispers that once filled my mind
The chaos that did steal my time
The darkness that did hold me tight
The voices that did tell me lies
The noise that was inside my head—
It's winding down
There's quiet now

Those who talked to me at length
Who called on me, who wished me strength
Those who came and gave me pills
My nerves to calm, dispel the chill
The ones who took the little notes—
They're all gone now
'Cause I've been found

The white walls that closed in on me
That kept me trapped, despite my pleas
The tiny room I spent my time
The space that I would long abide
The places where my demons lived—
I won't go back
It's time to pack

The promise of a brand-new day
The hope that darkness stays away
The light that found its way back in
The freedom from old ugly sin
The peace that only my heart knows—

FIVE DREAMS

I'm home again
With renewed soul

ELIZABETH MICHAUD

WIFE

He
will come
and take you
when you think not,
when you expect not;
you'll be a prisoner
of his sweet words; you'll be his
little toy; and the games he'll play
with you are not for the weak of heart—
your weak heart. He'll have your mind and your soul.

You will not flee; you'll belong to this man.
This wicked man who holds you captive.
He will whisper his lies to you,
over time you'll think them true.
True love, you will never
know; only pain and
only sorrow.
You'll be a
slave and
wife.

FIVE DREAMS

SPRING CLEANING

It's time to clean house.
It's time to rid my space of your shirts,
your shoes, your ties.
The pictures of you are no longer wanted;
they're cluttering my place,
and the trappings of your desires:
the women, the gambling, the pretty
bottles of Scotch—
I'm tossing them out with the trash.
Yes, it's time to clean house.
It's time to open the windows—
let the fresh air in!
This house smells of you:
the stink of your lies;
the reek of your betrayal;
the stench of your deceit.
Come in, spring breeze, and
clear the air—
I'm ready to breathe again.
Oh yes, let the cleaning begin!
It's time to chase the dark away.
You've left dreary in the corners,
and there's despair in the shades.
So I'll pull back the curtains and
let the sun shine in
to fade away the misery you left behind....
So I'll clean my house.
I'll change the sheets on the bed
and beat the rugs.

ELIZABETH MICHAUD

I'll put fresh flowers in the vases
and make the windows sparkle.
I'll sweep away the pain of your hurt,
and I'll dust away your memory.
And once my house is clean again,
I'll start my life anew,
without you.

I DREAM OF SORROW

ELIZABETH MICHAUD

FOR TANTE CECELLE

They tell me you're not here
and that we will no longer smell
the lingering smoke on your breath
or its faint tinge in your clothes
from your private smokes on the balcony
where you would not be disturbed

They tell me you're not here
and we will no longer hear
your jokes
the crass, sarcastic jokes that you told
when you cut your eyes
and sucked your tongue
when you were both annoyed and amused
at one, at all

They tell me you're not here
and we will no longer see
you traipsing about in your heels
your high heels
while you cleaned the kitchen or scrubbed the bathroom
because the flat, simple soles of slippers
hurt your back

They tell me that you're not here
no longer here
but they're wrong
because I know
when I catch scent of bitter, pungent smoke

FIVE DREAMS

and when I hear a naughty joke
or I see a pair of heels, high heels in a storefront
I will think of you
and you will be here
always here
forever here

ELIZABETH MICHAUD

REQUIEM FOR A WAKE

There is food in the house:
sitting, sitting
sitting out
on fancy plates
and laid out
on the table and 'round about;
there is food in the house.

There are folks in the house:
milling, milling
milling about
shuffling in
and shuffling out
in stiff attire they're clad about;
there are folks in the house.

There are flies in the house:
buzzing, buzzing
buzzing about
flying in
and flying out
through the door and 'round about;
there are flies in the house.

There is death in the house.
It creeps, it stalks
it lurks about
it sings a song, a triumphant shout!

FIVE DREAMS

While the food is sitting out
as the folks do mill about
and flies go buzzing in and out.
There is death in this house.

ELIZABETH MICHAUD

PUT FLOWERS ON MY GRAVE

Put flowers on my grave
and remember me softly
like petals on a flower
that bloom
that wither
that die

Put flowers on my grave
and say my name quietly
whisper it on the wind
with warmth
with love
with sadness

Put flowers on my grave
and wish for me gently
in the form of a prayer
for life
for love
for peace

Put flowers on my grave
but salt the earth of my remains
and shed not a tear for me
for I touched this place
and I walked this earth
and now my spirit's free
now my time moves on

FIVE DREAMS

So put flowers on my grave
because now I am gone

ELIZABETH MICHAUD

THE MEANINGLESS PROCESS OF GOODBYE

On the first day
they brought me their prayers;
their words did their slow dance
as their weight crushed me,
suffocated me.

On the second day
they brought me their sadness;
their tears rained down,
buckets of water drowning me,
drenching me.

On the third day
they brought me their flowers;
their grief decorated my grave
in vibrant color, irrelevant color
while my body lay in rot below.

FIVE DREAMS

TOO LITTLE, TOO LATE

Once when I did walk this earth
with quiet breath, with unsure step
I stood unseen, acknowledged not
among the masses, I mattered not
My words upon deaf ears did fall
with no concern, with no regard
My actions did not merit mark
not mere mention, or kind remark
And so when chance did come my way
I took a blade and cut away—

Now that I am far and gone
I watch them gather
I watch them come
at my grave, upon fresh earth
They mourn me softly
with cherished word
Many gather, stand side by side
send me a prayer through the skies—

In life they did not notice me
ignored my pain—a travesty!
But in loss their guilt is great;
ignored in life, revered in death
it is too late to repay the debt.

ELIZABETH MICHAUD

THE WISH OF A BATTERED SOUL

Weary as the day is long
I want to rest, to change this song
to sing a tune of angelic bliss
release my soul from this abyss
Wonder where new fortune lies
not on this earth—
    beyond the skies!
Somewhere far and so pristine
not this dark and dreary dream
Where here I perish, here I die
while looking for sweet lullaby
to set me on a brand-new course
escape this place, its harsh discourse
and let my soul soar yonder fast
into the heavens
home at last

FIVE DREAMS

ONCE IN FAITH

I believed once—
when my arms held my future:
a bundle of arms and legs that trembled and shook
and a tiny mouth that yearned for my mother's milk.

I believed once—
when I reveled in the sound of all my tomorrows:
of giggles and chuckles and the warm sound of laughter
as happy smiles sought my own.

I believed once—
when my eyes gazed upon all my great expectations:
on a life on the verge of great adventure,
with the breath of my blessings at her back.

I believed once—
even as a darkness lurked:
a threat that waited in shadows with ugly anticipation
as evil pervaded his thoughts.

I believed once—
until I looked at the face of my eternal hell:
the man who robbed me of my future,
stole all my tomorrows and shattered my great expectations.

I believed once—
when I said a prayer of goodbye:
a eulogy of promise for her life beyond this world,
her memory forever marking the point of my sorrow.

ELIZABETH MICHAUD

I believed—
  once.

FIVE DREAMS

GRIEF UNRELENTING

when once my eyes were closed in peace
I exhaled breath with rhythm deep
with touch of sun upon this place
and summer's breeze to bring its grace
a gentle strum of guitar strings
its song on air as if with wings—

when heartache breaks this solitude
an intermission, an interlude
here among these tombs of old
not even solace can be sold
I stand upon this hallowed ground
with tears of grief that know no bounds
and as my peace is stripped away
upon cold stone I beg and pray
to the gods I scream, I say
bring my lover back this day

ELIZABETH MICHAUD

GRIEF OF GHOSTS

In the quiet of the graveyard
in the quarter light of moon
fresh earth has yet to settle
and descend upon a tomb
She slips the bounds of earth
in search for one she missed
in search for her beloved
to free herself from this abyss—
And another soul does flitter
he wanders gently by
He's looking for his child
to whom he'll sing a lullaby—
And brother was a soldier
he carries still his gun
He's looking for the enemy
but here he finds there's none—
And the ghostly form of girl
wrists still crimson from her wounds
Who in life did dream of death
but now the darkness will impugn—
And further in the graveyard
under trees of pine and oak
other souls do gather
and wear night as their dark cloak
They whisper to each other
and the air will catch their grief
The living hear their cry
as moans and wails in night's soft breeze—

FIVE DREAMS

They're looking for their loved ones
They're looking for their lives
The ones who they believed in
and those they've left behind—
And in the quiet of the graveyard
in the quarter light of moon
they sing a song of sorrow
of lives gone much too soon.

I HAVE STRANGE DREAMS

ELIZABETH MICHAUD

IN THE EYE OF THE HEAVENLY STORM

While the moon continues to spin
and a comet streaks across the night,
Jupiter is rising but Saturn is descending;
solar flares erupt upon the sun,
explosions birth new planets,
and supernovas kill old stars.
Pluto wants to be seen but isn't,
and while the earth makes a year-long trek,
the constellations hold their nightly vigil.
Asteroids float lazily in the atmosphere,
and the moon plans to eclipse the sun.
A black hole engulfs the space around it,
meteors crash into planets,
and little brown dwarfs want to be orbs but aren't.
While Mercury is in retrograde,
and the North Star points the way,
the sun burns and scorches and warms,
and gravity fights to bring it all down but can't.
While the galaxy is in disarray,
while the universe is in constant chaos,
those two lovers in the night sky,
those two dueling celestial bodies,
Venus and Mars, are all right tonight.

TO THE WIND WITH GRATITUDE

When once the sun beat down on me,
and promised not a hint of mercy,
a gentle breeze began to blow
and dried the sweat from off my brow.
It tossed leaves high into the air,
and kites flew up with little care.
I raised my head for its touch of grace
while still sunlight caressed my face,
and in the wind I heard a call—

A gentle whisper floated by,
it seemed to me a lullaby:
"Watch as my wind makes light of day
and takes sun's heat so far away!"
And watch I did as through trees it blew,
the hair of ladies it tousled through.
It softened the strength of the summer sun,
and returned my promise of summer fun.
So to the wind: I thank you, my friend,
and with this I mark my verse's end.

ELIZABETH MICHAUD

GRAVE DIGGER

He toils for the dead.
He wears his hat
hung low on his brow.
It protects him from
the sun's harsh light;
It obscures his vision
from the task ahead.

He labors for the dead.
He carries a shovel
over his shoulder.
Its weight presses down,
digs in.
It reminds him that
he's still alive,
and there's important work
to be done.

He toils for the dead.
He seeks out a soft patch of earth,
and then he breaks ground.
He sweats as he digs
and the breaths he takes are shallow.
But he does take breath,
he does breathe.

FIVE DREAMS

He works for the dead.
But they pay him no fee.
He doesn't need a schedule,
he knows when to come in.
His employers do not speak,
but they trust in him,
as only they can.
He is their faithful servant.

He toils for the dead.
He prepares their final
resting place.
Then he sends them home.
It's a payment that he makes,
it's the tithe that he pays.
So that one day maybe,
perhaps,
someone will toil for him.

ELIZABETH MICHAUD

FACULTY MEETING

Sitting in a meeting
I watch the clock tick by
listening to the words they speak
but I do so wonder why;
this one says, "It's necessary...!"
that one gives the date,
and she's looking for some paperwork
'cause it "...can't be turned in late!"
He's planning the next meeting
and there's a conference yet ahead;
on and on and on they drone,
I wish I could be dead—
dead to endless meetings
and notes which matter not,
agendas that go nowhere
and the coffee hints of rot—
out beyond the window
there's freedom beyond reach;
escape from this dark dreary place
where I work and where I teach...
and still the meeting carries on,
and still the voices drone
as I picture myself gone
tucked away to my small home—
'til at last! The clock does chime the end,
it does extol the time
to end this dreary meeting
give me back my peace of mind;

FIVE DREAMS

so from the table, I do flee
and from this horror, I'll escape
'til this same time late next week:
another meeting we will take.

ELIZABETH MICHAUD

ACCIDENT

despite the wispy, silk-spun panels of clouds that stretched and
spread in the cerulean sky,
and tree branches that reached for each other
from either side of street; despite the lazy rays of sun
that shimmered from between those leafy lovers, and a cheeky breeze
that wouldn't fully commit to keeping one cool; despite
the audacity of tranquility on this little stretch of road,
rubber blackened and burned, metal crashed, twisted,
and screamed,
and glass shattered into a million tiny shards, into shiny diamond gems
with blood on their facets.

FIVE DREAMS

SHE WALKS THE GRAVEL ROAD

She walks the gravel road,
blue collar turned up against biting wind,
heavy orthopedics on her feet,
dragging loose pebbles,
kicking up dirt and dust and debris.
Her name tag says, "Mildred,"
an old name for an old woman,
tired from her long shift,
weary.
Fatigue droops her head;
gray hairs fray the bun and drape her face,
a lank, frizzy curtain.
Even her shoulders seek solace from the ground:
purse and bags and day's labor curve the back of the thin frame
and bring them down.

But she walks the gravel road,
the winding road, the twisty bend, the unfinished path;
joints creaking, feet aching,
but here, still here, for yet another day.

ELIZABETH MICHAUD

SIGHTLESS

Once when my eyes were lost to me
I saw as only the blind can see
I envisioned a life of roses and thorns
Of song and sermon
Right and wrong
And in my forever darkest night
I saw my world in glorious flight—

And when he with eyes that saw it all
Saw that I flew and did not fall
That in my blindness I was free
Released unbound
In ecstasy
I lived the life that I could not see—

When he with sight remarked my truth
Acknowledged that it was absolute
He saw his life devoid of use
Of love or passion
Or life's abuse—

Into his corner he so crept
Bowed his head and softly wept

THERE'S POETRY EVERYWHERE

Here, even here, in this humble abode
word and verse are hiding among the everyday:
in trees that cast their shadows
onto the faded curtain in front of the window,
and in the kitchen,
where the clink and tinkle of glasses being
put away can be heard;
in the sounds of rushing water from the open faucet
while dishes are being washed, and
around the table, where ghosts of conversations ebb and flow;
near the chimney, which makes a curious sound
when the wind bangs against it,
and in the soft pop and crackle of the fire that burns within—
secret stanzas with rhyme and meter lie
in wait even in the other room:
in sunlight that filters through the blinds
onto a terracotta wall, and
where dust settles on antique bottles
of wine and vinegar;
in the forgotten corners where the cobwebs dwell,
in the dying leaves of a neglected plant, and
among the books haplessly piled on the hardwood floor—
there are other places, too:
small snippets of chance and happenstance where
lyric and prose linger and loiter, biding their time;
inside the glimpse of an open door, where the bed is unmade
and clothes lay waste to the carpeted floor;
among the pictures on the walls, that gallery of memory and memento
in wooden frames, mounted both straight and askew;

in the quiet moan and groan of lovers in the back bedroom,
among the crash and crush of toy trucks and soldiers by little hands,
in the rustle of pages being turned in a book—

there's poetry everywhere

FIVE DREAMS

YOU TALK OF FREEDOM

You talk of freedom
and the rights of men
about how they trample on your rights
and suffocate your liberties—
"Down with tyranny!" I hear you say

But I can't even take a jog
through your neighborhood
and I can't kneel in protest
and I can't play with a toy gun
or eat a bag of skittles
while wearing a hoodie
on my way home

Yeah, you talk of freedom
and you cite the laws of the land—
"The founding fathers said *this*!"
and "The founding fathers said *that*!"

But I ain't free
not when I got
BBQ Becky in my face
and Permit Patty playing police
Pool Patrol Paula won't leave me in peace

Yeah, you talk about freedom
you carry your guns and you make your demands
waving signs of discontent highlighting your torment—
"Live free or die, you bastards! Live free or die!"

ELIZABETH MICHAUD

But I ain't got no choice
not even when my hands are up
or when I can't breathe
or when I don't even have a gun

Yeah, you talk of freedom
you cry about being free
but your freedom and your liberty
that don't apply to me

TRAGIC LIES

She stood before a mirror
and regarded her reflection.
She smiled at her image
for it was near perfection.
But behind her there he stood
to whisper a small lie:
"You are nothing, girl.
Of this, I won't deny."
But her spirit was too strong
and his words she'd not abide.

She stood before a mirror
and regarded her reflection.
The image was the same,
yet not so near perfection.
Behind her he stood there
to repeat his little lie:
"You are ugly, girl.
Of this, I won't deny."
Her spirit now was weaker
and tears slipped from her eyes.

She stood before a mirror
and regarded her reflection,
with eyes that still shone true
but now she saw the imperfections.
Behind her still he stood
and again he told his lie:

ELIZABETH MICHAUD

"You are no one, girl.
Of this, I won't deny."
Her spirit was now broken
and she thought to take her life.

She stood before a mirror
and her reflection she detected:
a ghostly image pale and faint
of the life that she rejected.
He stood in the glass,
still behind her as before
to whisper words so cruel and true
as she floated out the door:
"Oh, lovely little girl you were,
now you are no more."

FIVE DREAMS

A SUMMER GATHERING

A birthday for the
boy with buddies. There's
cake to decorate; we'll
delicately and dutifully
embellish it with edible
flowers and the
girls will laugh and celebrate. We'll
have our summer fete with
ice cream and smores under
juniper trees and the aroma of
kabobs roasting on the grill. The
little ones will play games with
monsters hiding in trees or
nab fireflies in the dwindling light;
over beer and sweet tea,
parents will
quote lyrics from old songs and
reminisce about
summers past and gone.
Time slips quickly and someone takes out a
ukulele and strums
virtually any silly tune to a drunken chorus—
will wonders never cease? We'll sit on
xenolithic rocks of old, around a campfire,
youth passing us by, but still at the
zenith of our lives.

NIGHTMARES

ELIZABETH MICHAUD

GHOST

Moan and wail, clank of chain
Smell of death, recall pain
Haunts this hall, brings on fright
Shackled man who lurks this night

Smoke and mist, trick of light
Floats on air, a ghastly sight
Behind glass, through the door
Children, hide! And look no more

Obscure face, unknown soul
Wanders past, wanders slow
Sudden chill, horrid gasp
How long shall this terror last?

Rambles through, seeks to find
Passage to another time
Bloodless spirit forced to dwell
Here on earth, a ghostly shell

Shimmers dark, shimmers light
Brings on fear, shrieks at night
Children, flee! Run and hide
'Lest your wish too is to die

Beast and fiend, man no more
Soul is gone, love abhors
Anger stirs, hope is lost
Demon creature will accost

FIVE DREAMS

Children, please! Heed this cry
For this is no lullaby
Rage abounds, fury too
Care that he comes not for you

Moan and wail, clank of chain
Near the end of terror's reign
Takes a soul, guards it well
Floats them both on down to hell.

ELIZABETH MICHAUD

THE WIND IS HIS MESSENGER

Wind howls at my window
and shrieks a little more
it rattles against
        the windowpane
an ill and frightening score

Night cloaks its intentions
darkness is its friend
it screams its way
        through silent trees
I sense my time at end

The wind is *his* apprentice
it does as it is told
it whips a message
        through the air
and makes my blood run cold

The wind will do his bidding
it's calling out my name
it seeks for me
        this horrid night
it knows my guilt and shame

It's building up a fury
it's angry—don't you see
its screech is strong
        and high with might
it's coming after me

FIVE DREAMS

So I dig a little deeper
'neath the blankets of my bed
I wish for some assistance
with this sense of fear and dread

'Cause the wind is a suggestion
it hints at something more
the devil comes for me this night
the wind blares his great horn

LET THE SOUNDS BE A WARNING

Listen, children, to this night,
It bears a warning of great fright.
The boom of thunder is fanfare
To night's terror: Hark! Beware!

Hear not you the demons stroll?
With menace creep, with menace roam.
Lightening cracks—oh children see!
Horrid things will come for thee!

Sounds abound and pierce the dark,
Creatures come to leave their mark.
Phantoms wail and monsters too,
A wolfhound howls—
        It honors moon.

Tombs creak open:
        Hear scratch and scrape!
Untold horrors make quick escape.
Groans emit from these undead;
        It brings forth fear,
        It brings forth dread—

The witch's cackle is oft heard
And black crows caw,
Their sound absurd—
        Death is inferred.
Ghouls and goblins swear and hiss;
Evil's night is their sweet bliss.

FIVE DREAMS

But behold this night song's end;
Do take heed of word I send.
The final sound we've yet to hear:
      A scream of death;
      A scream of fear.

Run, run children! Flee and hide!
Before the sounds are by your side.

ELIZABETH MICHAUD

THE NAMING OF HER

The night begins with darkest spell
She calls forth demons from deepest hell
She sends them out to do her will
They venture off into night's chill

They set about in secret search
Upon the shadows they hunch, they lurch
Their mistress's wish they do fulfill
And bring to her much treasured ills

A pint of blood, a pound of flesh
A heart ripped from a tender chest
Screams of children bottled tight
And eyes bereft of all their sight

With incantation now complete
With black cat purring at her feet
An evil bidding stirs her soul
Intent as dark and black as coal

She chants her words for all to hear
And one by one, they fall in fear
Her whispered words consume them all
She stands, she laughs, she lets them fall

With her curse her victims writhe
Her spell a scourge by which they'll die
The night is pierced by screams and pleas
Their wretched souls are hers to seize

FIVE DREAMS

And with her bounty of skin and bone
With withered souls that moan and groan
She steals her way into the night
And cackles oft with all her might

To her dark prince of down below
These bloody gifts she does bestow
For evil's trouble he grants a wish
He calls her hag, trickster, and

Witch.

ELIZABETH MICHAUD

THE DEVIL'S HARLOT

There is a whisper that they speak
Of one so lovely, of beauty deep
She who stands with skin so fair
Eyes aglow and silken hair
And so they whisper with much lust
Of soft caress and passion's touch

But men are men as men can be
And turn blind eye to what they see
Behind this mask of golden face
There hides a soul of spite and hate
Of venom pure, deceit so foul
Men! Beware of lover's scowl

There is no goodness to be found
There is no virtue that abounds
The beauty inside is but a wish
The dream of men, a tasty dish

Oh, men, oh men! Why know they not?
She lies in wait, she spins her plot
And with a savage cold hard hand
She strikes them down, she strikes down men
And sends them to her maker's feast
Where he dines on tasty treats

FIVE DREAMS

BLACK WIDOW

A bit of poison on the tongue
Or prick of knife upon the chest
Will bring down her lover's heart
And help him find eternal rest—

Wedding vow will now stand broken
"Love forever" will not be kept
Bride is free to find another
And build anew her lover's nest—

'Til at last she does grow weary
And bond of love becomes no more
She'll seek to find another mate
For after all, she is a whore—

A whore for love and title too
She longs to stand and say "I do"
A million times and ten times more
Until love's union is a chore—

And so she'll spill his blood anew
Then shed false tears with grief untrue
Bid adieu, give kiss goodbye
Touch cold cheek and eulogize—

Oh murd'rous woman! wife and fiend
She knows no guilt, her shame unseen
She'll kill each man with whom she shared
A solemn vow, an oath to care—

And then move on her wicked way
To play *dear wife* another day.

FIVE DREAMS

RAT

In the corner there's a rat,
he sits there watching me:
tattooed, scarred, and worst of all
dirty as can be.
He knows all my secrets,
I can see it in his eyes,
and when the moment comes along,
he'll betray me with his lies—
He'll whisper to another
the things they need to hear:
dates and times and places
of the acts committed here—

He's plotting my demise,
it's the cost of his release;
the price he'll pay for freedom
is this treachery towards me.
This cell is way too small
for the two of us to share,
so when justice knocks upon the door,
it's the cloak of truth he'll wear—

But before they come to take me,
before they take my life,
I'll set a little poison,
I'll draw out my knife.
This man who was a traitor,
who served me up to them,
I'll spill his blood upon the floor—

it'll be the death of him.
And I'll bide my time,
a mighty victor in my cell.
Guard my secret well, my friend,
or you too I'll send to hell.

FIVE DREAMS

INTRUDER

There's a knock upon my door
Despite the lateness of the hour
From this sound I turn my ear
And step away a little further
From the stranger who awaits me
On the other side of the door—

I ponder his desire
But I do fear his intentions
So I leave the door unanswered
I wish for more modest conventions
But the knock does come again
With a force a little harder—

I pose a question to the stranger
But an answer comes forth not
Just a greater sense of danger
Fear begins to seize my heart—

And the knock becomes a pounding
A multitude of fists
Door trembles, shakes, and shudders
What is this curious twist?

To the man, I ask a question
Who does beat down my door
He seeks an entry to my home
To shatter my abode
I shout a question of this man

ELIZABETH MICHAUD

    (Or perhaps he is a beast)
What it is his heart demands
What it is he wants of me?

But no answer yet is given
And the pounding is a clamor
I feel a shudder in my heart
My speech begins to stammer—

I shriek a question to the creature
Won't you please sir leave me be
I seek peace and solace on this night
I do wish not for company—

But the man who is a demon
As his intent from hell must come
Refuses my request
        My words to him are merely jest—

And the banging does continue
'Til a crack shows in the door
'Til the frame once strong is shattered
And I feel my breath no more—

Through my door which is now broken
Through the threshold, he does step
I now stand in utter terror
I'm loathe to hear his manifest—

A knife gleams in his hand
And he holds it up so high

FIVE DREAMS

It shines with menace from the light
And there is evil in his eyes—

I beg and plead for a response
To my question from before
And as I scream a desperate prayer
For some help from this dark strife
He looks at me and does respond—

I've come to take your life.

AND AN ANGEL WILL LEAD HIM HOME

When once was lost a good man's soul
and he renounced the promised home
when darkness pushed the light away
he vowed he would no longer play
when rules and law, they mattered not—
he sought a new way home.

When his conscience led him not
and the words he prayed were all for naught
when God did turn his back on him
his hands were covered in blood of kin
when guilt for him held no concern—
he sought a new way home.

When once the love this man did hold
changed in tenor and in code
when he invited evil in
when he committed grievous sin
when he spilled the blood of a humble man—
he sought a new way home.

When once an angel of netherworld
ventured forth and spoke a word
the angel made a promise true
of a place of blackest hue
where fires burned in name of sin—
he found a new way home.

FIVE DREAMS

LAST WORDS

Ain't gonna be no tombstone where I lie—
but I don't need one.
My story is too big
for your piece of wood anyway.
You think 'cause you gonna put me
in a plain old box, nobody knows me?
People gonna forget me?
Please.
Everybody knows me.
And they're *all* gonna remember me.
The things I've done, the people
I've hurt, the folks I killed—
I'm infamous.
So you can drop me in here if you want to
and walk away like it don't matter
—'cause it don't—
but long after I'm done here,
they'll still be talking about me,
even when
weeds done covered my plot of earth
and my unmarked grave is gone.

Printed in the USA
CPSIA information can be obtained
at www.ICGtesting.com
JSHW020302220224
57830JS00006B/62